ISBN: 978-1-964400-28-0

Designed by: Ruth Fleury

Email: s.o.tpublishing@gmail.com

Printed in the United States of America

Dedication

I dedicate this journal to every woman who has ever felt unseen, unheard, or unloved.

May these pages remind you of your worth, your strength, and your power to set boundaries, to heal, and to embrace love...beginning with yourself.

To my daughters and every future generation: may you always know that flourishing is not about perfection, but about growing in peace, walking in purpose, and choosing love every day.

With love and gratitude, Ruth Fleury

Dear Beautiful lady,

This journal was created with you in mind, the woman who has carried so much, given so much, and yet still chooses to rise, heal, and love again.

As women, we often pour into others until we are empty. This journal is your reminder that you, too, deserve space to breathe, reflect, and be poured into. Within these pages, you'll find guided prompts, affirmations, and room for your own words, each one designed to help you:

- Heal from what no longer serves you.
- Set boundaries that honor your peace.
- Embrace the fullness of self-love.
- Build memories and a legacy of love for generations to come.

Know this: your healing matters. Your boundaries matter. Your love matters. And most importantly, you matter. God is still in control, and He is guiding you through this journey.

Take your time with these pages. Write when you feel led. Cry if you must. Celebrate your breakthroughs. Allow this journal to be your safe space, a companion that reminds you of your worth, your strength, and your beautiful ability to flourish.

With love, peace, and faith,

Ruth Fleury

Before You Begin

Take a deep breath.

(Breathe in positive energy through your nose, hold for 4 seconds then breathe out the negative energy)

Release the weight of yesterday.

Open your heart to what God has for you today.

Prayer of purpose and mindful journey

"Lord, as I step into these pages, quiet my mind and calm my spirit.

Help me to release the things that hurt, embrace the lessons that heal, and trust Your hand guiding my journey.

Let every word I write draw me closer to peace, purpose, and love. Amen."

Affirmation to Begin

I am safe here.

My voice matters.

My healing matters.

With each page,

I flourish in love,

guided by faith and grace.

Healing

A space to release, reflect, and renew.

Prompts

- What past wound am I ready to release today?

- In what ways has pain shaped me into the woman I am becoming?

- How can I invite God's peace into the places that still hurt?

Healing Affirmations

- I am healing at my own pace, and that is enough.

- God's love restores my heart and mind.

- My scars are reminders of my strength, not my limits.

Boundaries

A space to protect your peace and honor your worth.

Prompts

- What boundary do I need to set to protect my energy?

- How do I feel when someone respects my boundaries?

- Write about a time you struggled to say "no." How can you honor yourself differently now?

Boundaries Affirmations

- My boundaries are acts of self-love and self-respect.

- It is safe to put myself first when I need to.

- I teach others how to love me by the way I love myself.

Love

A space to nurture self-love, relationships, and connection.

Prompts

- Write a love letter to yourself.

- Who in my life makes me feel safe, valued, and supported?

- How can I show love to someone in my family today?

Love Affirmations

- I am worthy of love, exactly as I am.

- I choose love over fear every day.

- Love surrounds me, flows through me, and flourishes within me.

Legacy

A space to build memories and pass love forward.

Prompts

- What legacy of love do I want to leave for my children, family, or community?

- What is one tradition or memory I want to create this year?

- How do I want to be remembered for the way I love?

Legacy Affirmations

- I am planting seeds of love that will outlive me.

- The memories I create today are treasures for tomorrow.

- My life is a legacy of healing, boundaries, and love.

Ruth Fleury's Words of Wisdom

"Be obedient as the chosen one to walk in your purpose and shine light for others to be inspired to find their why."

"Every time you rise, you give someone else permission to believe it's possible." "Even in challenge, joy is your superpower. Use it daily."

"Let joy be your resistance and purpose your response."

"Self-belief is the spark, reflection is the mirror, and consistency is the engine that gets you to your dream."

"You don't have to be perfect- just present, patient, and persistent." "Plant peace, speak love, and watch the world bloom, one heart at a time."

"Stay coachable. Listen with intention. Capture the wisdom. Reflect on it. Then go out and create something extraordinary."

"Let your joy be loud, and your growth be louder. Keep smiling and thriving!"

Ruth Fleury, M.S. Ed

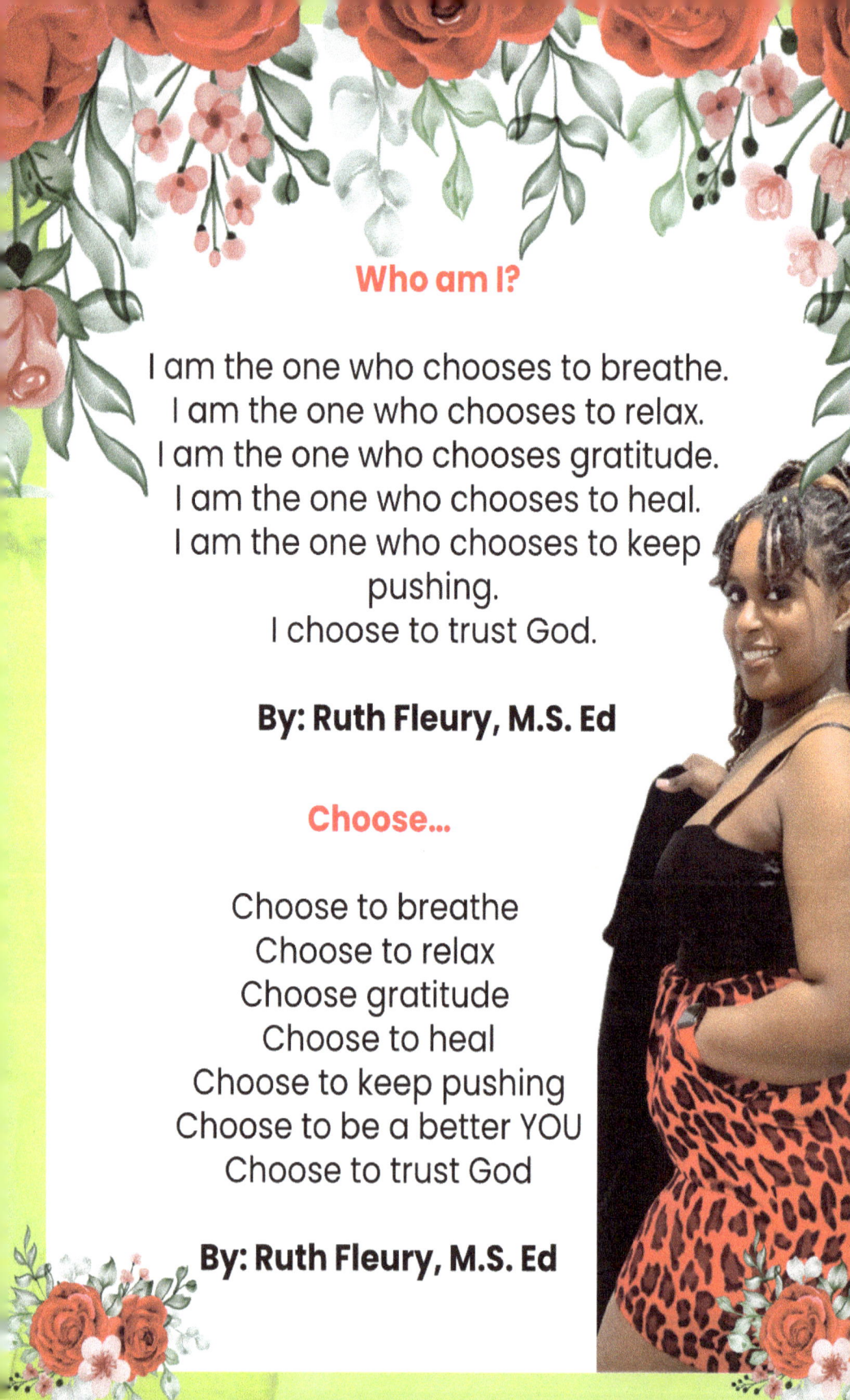

Who am I?

I am the one who chooses to breathe.
I am the one who chooses to relax.
I am the one who chooses gratitude.
I am the one who chooses to heal.
I am the one who chooses to keep pushing.
I choose to trust God.

By: Ruth Fleury, M.S. Ed

Choose...

Choose to breathe
Choose to relax
Choose gratitude
Choose to heal
Choose to keep pushing
Choose to be a better YOU
Choose to trust God

By: Ruth Fleury, M.S. Ed

Today's date: _____

_____

_____

_____

_____

_____

_____

_____

_____

_____

_____

_____

_____

_____

_____

_____

_____

_____

_____

_____

_____

_____

_____

_____

# Psalm 23

1 The Lord is my shepherd, I lack nothing.
2 He makes me lie down in green pastures,
he leads me beside quiet waters,
3 he refreshes my soul.
He guides me along the right paths
for his name's sake.
4 Even though I walk
through the darkest valley,
I will fear no evil,
for you are with me;
your rod and your staff,
they comfort me.
5 You prepare a table before me
in the presence of my enemies.
You anoint my head with oil;
my cup overflows.
6 Surely your goodness and love will follow me
all the days of my life,
and I will dwell in the house of the Lord
forever.

BIBLE

VERSE

Psalms 23

" 1 The Lord is my shepherd, I lack nothing.
2 He makes me lie down in green pastures,
he leads me beside quiet waters,
3 he refreshes my soul..."

REFLECTION

_____

_____

_____

_____

_____

_____

_____

BIBLE VERSE

Your Bible verse: _

_____

_____

_____

_____

_____

_____

January

Claim Your Space...

Claim Your Space means to release what no longer serves you:

physically,

emotionally,

energetically

It's the gentle but powerful act of creating room in your life for:

peace,

purpose,

possibility

It looks like:

- Letting go of clutter that drains your energy
- Releasing toxic thoughts, habits, or relationships
- Saying "no" so you can say "yes" to yourself
- Creating quiet moments to breathe, feel, and realign Clearing your space is not about perfection, it's about permission.

Permission to grow.

To heal.

To come back to yourself.

BIBLE VERSE

Your Bible verse: _

_____

_____

_____

_____

_____

_____

_____

January

Claim Your Space

Theme: Ownership, clarity, intention

1. Am I still seeking external validation instead of trusting my own voice?

Today's date: _____

January

Claim Your Space

Theme: Ownership, clarity, intention

2. What do I want this year to feel like?

Today's date: _____

WELLNESS JOURNAL

DATE:

MORNING ROUTINE:

- ☐ WAKE UP EARLY
- ☐ PRACTICE DEEP BREATHING FOR 3-5 MIN.
- ☐ HYDRATE WITH A GLASS OF WATER
- ☐ STRETCH

PHYSICAL ACTIVITY:

- ☐ ENGAGE IN 30 MINUTES OF EXERCISE
- ☐ TAKE SHORT WALKS OR STRETCH BREAKS
- ☐ USE THE STAIRS INSTEAD OF THE ELEVATOR
- ☐ TRACK DAILY STEPS

SELF-CARE:

- ☐ SET BOUNDARIES FOR YOUR PERSONAL TIME
- ☐ DO SOMETHING YOU ENJOY FOR AT LEAST 15 MIN.
- ☐ TAKE SHORT BREAKS TO RELAX
- ☐ DISCONNECT FROM SCREENS AT LEAST AN
  HOUR BEFORE BED

WATER INTAKE:

GRATITUDE:

- ☐ I'M GRATEFUL FOR MY HEALTH
- ☐ I APPRECIATE MY LOVED ONES
- ☐ I'M THANKFUL FOR LIFE
- ☐ I'M GRATEFUL FOR NEW OPPORTUNITIES

MINDFULNESS:

- ☐ 10 MINUTES OF MEDITATION
- ☐ GRATITUDE JOURNALING
- ☐ TAKE A FEW SOFT AND DEEP BREATHS
- ☐ MINDFUL EATING DURING MEALS

REFLECTION:

- ☐ REFLECT ON YOUR ACHIEVEMENTS TODAY
- ☐ NOTE ANY CHALLENGES
- ☐ HOW YOU OVERCAME THEM
- ☐ SET A SMALL WELLNESS GOAL FOR TOMORR

NUTRITION:

- ☐ EAT A BALANCED BREAKFAST
- ☐ PLAN HEALTHY MEALS FOR THE DAY
- ☐ SNACK ON FRUITS OR NUTS
- ☐ STAY HYDRATED THROUGHOUT THE DAY

NOTES:

January

Claim Your Space

Theme: Ownership, clarity, intention

3. What do I need to stop shrinking for and focus more on producing?

Today's date: ——————————

January

Claim Your Space

Theme: Ownership, clarity, intention

4. What habits are you ready to let go of?

Today's date: _____

_____

_____

_____

_____

_____

_____

_____

_____

_____

_____

_____

_____

_____

_____

_____

_____

_____

_____

_____

_____

_____

_____

January

Claim Your Space

Theme: Ownership, clarity, intention

5. What would it mean to truly own my voice, body, or story?

Today's date: _____

Dice Brain Break

Roll a dice. The number that it lands on corresponds with the brain break activity!

	Dance for a one minute!
	Look in the mirror for two minutes!
	Take three deep breaths!
	Do four jumping jacks!
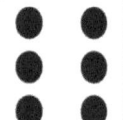	Do five leg ups.
	Jog in place and count to 6.

Take care of yourself first

Self Care Ideas

Spa day
Solo date
See a therapist
Read a book
Write in your journal
Run daily/weekly
Walk or go to the gym
Go to the hair salon or nail salon
Go on a date with a family or friend

date night

Effective Action Plan

1 Define Your Objectives

2 Set Your Goals

3 Prepare a Visual Plan

4 Assess Your Resources

5 Watch, Reflect, and Update

Effective Action Plan

February

Sacred Self-Love

Sacred self-love is the deep, unconditional acceptance of who you are: mind, body, heart, spirit.

It's not just about bubble baths or beauty rituals. It's about honoring yourself as worthy, whole, and divine (exactly as you are).

It's the way you speak to yourself when no one's listening.

It's setting boundaries without guilt.

It's showing up for yourself, especially on the days when it feels difficult.

It's knowing your value doesn't depend on your productivity or your past.

Sacred self-love is a lifelong relationship—with grace, with healing, and with your own radiant truth.

BIBLE
VERSE

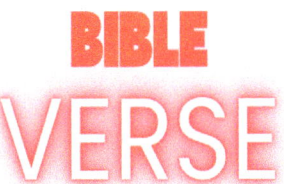

our Bible verse: _

REFLECTION

_____

_____

_____

_____

_____

_____

_____

February

Sacred Self-Love

Theme: Compassion, boundaries, redefining care

1. How do I define love and how does that shape my choices?

Today's date: _____

_____
_____
_____
_____
_____
_____
_____
_____
_____
_____
_____
_____
_____
_____
_____
_____
_____
_____
_____
_____
_____
_____

February

Sacred Self-Love

Theme: Compassion, boundaries, redefining care

2. Where have I confused love with self-sacrifice?

Today's date: _____

WELLNESS JOURNAL

DATE: ....

MORNING ROUTINE:

- ☐ WAKE UP EARLY
- ☐ PRACTICE DEEP BREATHING FOR 3-5 MIN.
- ☐ HYDRATE WITH A GLASS OF WATER
- ☐ STRETCH

PHYSICAL ACTIVITY:

- ☐ ENGAGE IN 30 MINUTES OF EXERCISE
- ☐ TAKE SHORT WALKS OR STRETCH BREAKS
- ☐ USE THE STAIRS INSTEAD OF THE ELEVATOR
- ☐ TRACK DAILY STEPS

SELF-CARE:

- ☐ SET BOUNDARIES FOR YOUR PERSONAL TIME
- ☐ DO SOMETHING YOU ENJOY FOR AT LEAST 15 MIN.
- ☐ TAKE SHORT BREAKS TO RELAX
- ☐ DISCONNECT FROM SCREENS AT LEAST AN HOUR BEFORE BED

WATER INTAKE:

◇ ◇ ◇ ◇ ◇
◇ ◇ ◇ ◇ ◇

GRATITUDE:

- ☐ I'M GRATEFUL FOR MY HEALTH
- ☐ I APPRECIATE MY LOVED ONES
- ☐ I'M THANKFUL FOR LIFE
- ☐ I'M GRATEFUL FOR NEW OPPORTUNITIES

MINDFULNESS:

- ☐ 10 MINUTES OF MEDITATION
- ☐ GRATITUDE JOURNALING
- ☐ TAKE A FEW SOFT AND DEEP BREATHS
- ☐ MINDFUL EATING DURING MEALS

REFLECTION:

- ☐ REFLECT ON YOUR ACHIEVEMENTS TODAY
- ☐ NOTE ANY CHALLENGES
- ☐ HOW YOU OVERCAME THEM
- ☐ SET A SMALL WELLNESS GOAL FOR TOMORR

NUTRITION:

- ☐ EAT A BALANCED BREAKFAST
- ☐ PLAN HEALTHY MEALS FOR THE DAY
- ☐ SNACK ON FRUITS OR NUTS
- ☐ STAY HYDRATED THROUGHOUT THE DAY

NOTES:

- •
- •
- •

Take care of yourself first

Self Care Ideas

Spa day
Solo date
See a therapist
Read a book
Write in your journal
Run daily/weekly
Walk or go to the gym
Go to the hair salon or nail salon
Go on a date with a family or friend

February

Sacred Self-Love

Theme: Compassion, boundaries, redefining care

3. What does love from me to me look like in action?

Today's date: —————————

February

Sacred Self-Love

Theme: Compassion, boundaries, redefining care

4. Where do I need to draw a loving boundary?

Today's date: _____

February

Sacred Self-Love

Theme: Compassion, boundaries, redefining care

5. What kind of love am I ready to receive?

Today's date: _____

_____

_____

_____

_____

_____

_____

_____

_____

_____

_____

_____

_____

_____

_____

_____

_____

_____

_____

_____

Effective Action Plan

1 Define Your Objectives

2 Set Your Goals

3 Prepare a Visual Plan

4 Assess Your Resources

5 Watch, Reflect, and Update

Effective Action Plan

March

Trust the Timing

Theme: Patience, Surrender, Faith

"Trust the Timing" is an invitation to lean into patience, release control, and believe that what is meant for you will unfold at the right moment. It reminds us that life is not a race and that our journeys don't have to mirror anyone else's.

Patience teaches us to slow down and appreciate the process instead of rushing toward outcomes. Growth, healing, and transformation take time — just like a seed planted in the soil needs to root before it blooms.

Surrender asks us to let go of the constant need to force things into place. When we surrender, we allow life to guide us rather than stressing over every detail. Surrender doesn't mean giving up; it means creating space for clarity, alignment, and ease.

Faith is the belief that even when things feel uncertain or delayed, the universe is still working for your good. Faith carries you through the in-between moments — the waiting, the wondering, the becoming.

To "Trust the Timing" is to honor your own pace, believe in your own story, and know deeply that what is meant for you will never miss you. It's a gentle reminder: Everything unfolds exactly when you're ready.

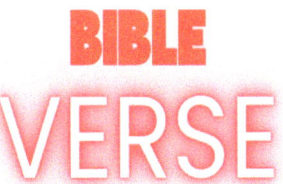

BIBLE VERSE

Your Bible verse: _____

REFLECTION

_____

_____

_____

_____

_____

_____

_____

March

Trust the Timing

Theme: Patience, Surrender, Faith

1. Where do I feel rushed? Why?

Today's date: _____

March

Trust the Timing

Theme: Patience, Surrender, Faith

2. What am I forcing instead of allowing?

Today's date: _____

_____
_____
_____
_____
_____
_____
_____
_____
_____
_____
_____
_____
_____
_____
_____
_____
_____
_____
_____
_____
_____
_____

WELLNESS JOURNAL

DATE: _____

MORNING ROUTINE:

- ☐ WAKE UP EARLY
- ☐ PRACTICE DEEP BREATHING FOR 3-5 MIN.
- ☐ HYDRATE WITH A GLASS OF WATER
- ☐ STRETCH

PHYSICAL ACTIVITY:

- ☐ ENGAGE IN 30 MINUTES OF EXERCISE
- ☐ TAKE SHORT WALKS OR STRETCH BREAKS
- ☐ USE THE STAIRS INSTEAD OF THE ELEVATOR
- ☐ TRACK DAILY STEPS

SELF-CARE:

- ☐ SET BOUNDARIES FOR YOUR PERSONAL TIME
- ☐ DO SOMETHING YOU ENJOY FOR AT LEAST 15 MIN.
- ☐ TAKE SHORT BREAKS TO RELAX
- ☐ DISCONNECT FROM SCREENS AT LEAST AN
  HOUR BEFORE BED

WATER INTAKE:

GRATITUDE:

- ☐ I'M GRATEFUL FOR MY HEALTH
- ☐ I APPRECIATE MY LOVED ONES
- ☐ I'M THANKFUL FOR LIFE
- ☐ I'M GRATEFUL FOR NEW OPPORTUNITIES

MINDFULNESS:

- ☐ 10 MINUTES OF MEDITATION
- ☐ GRATITUDE JOURNALING
- ☐ TAKE A FEW SOFT AND DEEP BREATHS
- ☐ MINDFUL EATING DURING MEALS

REFLECTION:

- ☐ REFLECT ON YOUR ACHIEVEMENTS TODAY
- ☐ NOTE ANY CHALLENGES
- ☐ HOW YOU OVERCAME THEM
- ☐ SET A SMALL WELLNESS GOAL FOR TOMOR

NUTRITION:

- ☐ EAT A BALANCED BREAKFAST
- ☐ PLAN HEALTHY MEALS FOR THE DAY
- ☐ SNACK ON FRUITS OR NUTS
- ☐ STAY HYDRATED THROUGHOUT THE DAY

NOTES:

Take care of yourself first

Self Care Ideas

Spa day
Solo date
See a therapist
Read a book
Write in your journal
Run daily/weekly
Walk or go to the gym
Go to the hair salon or nail salon
Go on a date with a family or friend

March

Trust the Timing

Theme: Patience, Surrender, Faith

3. How can I trust that what's meant for me is unfolding?

Today's date: _____

_____
_____
_____
_____
_____
_____
_____
_____
_____
_____
_____
_____
_____
_____
_____
_____
_____
_____
_____
_____
_____

March

Trust the Timing

Theme: Patience, Surrender, Faith

4. What's something I've outgrown, but haven't let go of?

Today's date: _____

_____
_____
_____
_____
_____
_____
_____
_____
_____
_____
_____
_____
_____
_____
_____
_____
_____
_____
_____
_____
_____
_____
_____
_____

March

Trust the Timing

Theme: Patience, Surrender, Faith

5. In what ways can I loosen my grip and gently lean into the natural flow of my life?

Today's date: _____

_____

_____

_____

_____

_____

_____

_____

_____

_____

_____

_____

_____

_____

_____

_____

_____

_____

_____

_____

_____

Share your Thoughts

Effective Action Plan

1 Define Your Objectives

2 Set Your Goals

3 Prepare a Visual Plan

4 Assess Your Resources

5 Watch, Reflect, and Update

Effective Action Plan

April

The Art of Shedding

"The Art of Shedding" is the intentional practice of letting go: of weight, worries, habits, and identities that no longer align with the woman you're becoming. Just like nature releases old leaves to make space for new growth, shedding is a sacred act of clearing room for clarity and transformation.

Clarity arrives when you begin to see what is truly serving you and what is silently holding you back. Shedding helps you remove the noise like old stories, limiting beliefs, and emotional clutter, so you can finally recognize your deeper truth.

Release is the courageous process of loosening your grip on what once felt familiar but now feels heavy. Releasing doesn't happen all at once; it's a gentle, ongoing unfolding. Every time you release something that no longer fits your spirit, you reclaim energy, space, and freedom.

Transformation is the natural result of shedding. When you let go of what burdens you, you rise into a stronger, clearer, more aligned version of yourself. Transformation happens not because you force it, but because you honor what needs to fall away.

"The Art of Shedding" reminds you that growth is not just about adding more to your life, it's about removing what blocks your light. It is a journey of becoming lighter, wiser, and more deeply grounded in who you truly are.

BIBLE VERSE

Your Bible verse: _____

REFLECTION

_____

_____

_____

_____

_____

_____

April

The Art of Shedding

Theme: Clarity, Release, transformation

1. What truths about my journey have begun to reveal themselves more clearly lately?

Today's date: _____

April

The Art of Shedding

Theme: Clarity, Release, transformation

2. What am I still holding onto that no longer aligns with my growth or who I'm becoming?

Today's date: _____

WELLNESS JOURNAL

DATE: _____

MORNING ROUTINE:

- [ ] WAKE UP EARLY
- [ ] PRACTICE DEEP BREATHING FOR 3-5 MIN.
- [ ] HYDRATE WITH A GLASS OF WATER
- [ ] STRETCH

PHYSICAL ACTIVITY:

- [ ] ENGAGE IN 30 MINUTES OF EXERCISE
- [ ] TAKE SHORT WALKS OR STRETCH BREAKS
- [ ] USE THE STAIRS INSTEAD OF THE ELEVATOR
- [ ] TRACK DAILY STEPS

SELF-CARE:

- [ ] SET BOUNDARIES FOR YOUR PERSONAL TIME
- [ ] DO SOMETHING YOU ENJOY FOR AT LEAST 15 MIN.
- [ ] TAKE SHORT BREAKS TO RELAX
- [ ] DISCONNECT FROM SCREENS AT LEAST AN HOUR BEFORE BED

WATER INTAKE:

GRATITUDE:

- [ ] I'M GRATEFUL FOR MY HEALTH
- [ ] I APPRECIATE MY LOVED ONES
- [ ] I'M THANKFUL FOR LIFE
- [ ] I'M GRATEFUL FOR NEW OPPORTUNITIES

MINDFULNESS:

- [ ] 10 MINUTES OF MEDITATION
- [ ] GRATITUDE JOURNALING
- [ ] TAKE A FEW SOFT AND DEEP BREATHS
- [ ] MINDFUL EATING DURING MEALS

REFLECTION:

- [ ] REFLECT ON YOUR ACHIEVEMENTS TODAY
- [ ] NOTE ANY CHALLENGES
- [ ] HOW YOU OVERCAME THEM
- [ ] SET A SMALL WELLNESS GOAL FOR TOMORR

NUTRITION:

- [ ] EAT A BALANCED BREAKFAST
- [ ] PLAN HEALTHY MEALS FOR THE DAY
- [ ] SNACK ON FRUITS OR NUTS
- [ ] STAY HYDRATED THROUGHOUT THE DAY

NOTES:

- _____
- _____
- _____

Take care of yourself first

Self Care Ideas

Spa day
Solo date
See a therapist
Read a book
Write in your journal
Run daily/weekly
Walk or go to the gym
Go to the hair salon or nail salon
Go on a date with a family or friend

April

The Art of Shedding

Theme: Clarity, Release, transformation

3. What seeds am I ready to plant this month that will grow into meaningful change in my life?

Today's date: ———————————

April

The Art of Shedding

Theme: Clarity, Release, transformation

4. Where in my life am I out of alignment with my values?

Today's date: _____

_____

_____

_____

_____

_____

_____

_____

_____

_____

_____

_____

_____

_____

_____

_____

_____

_____

_____

_____

_____

_____

April

The Art of Shedding

Theme: Clarity, Release, transformation

5. What small shift can I make today that aligns with the person I am becoming?

Today's date: ———————————

Effective Action Plan

1 Define Your Objectives

2 Set Your Goals

3 Prepare a Visual Plan

4 Assess Your Resources

5 Watch, Reflect, and Update

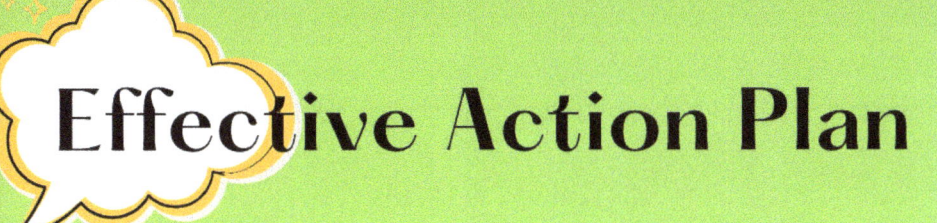

Effective Action Plan

May

Nourish to Flourish

Theme: Self-Care, Restoration, Body Wisdom

"Nourish to Flourish" is a reminder that growth, joy, and fulfillment come from the way you care for yourself: mind, body, and spirit. It teaches that flourishing isn't something you hustle your way into; it's something you grow into when you consistently choose nourishment.

Self-care is the foundation. Nourishment begins with honoring your needs like resting before you burn out, saying no when something drains you, and making time for what brings you peace and pleasure. Self-care is not selfish; it's essential fuel for your well-being.

Restoration is the healing stage. It's the intentional act of returning to yourself after life's demands have stretched you thin. Restoration looks like quiet moments, gentle routines, deep breaths, and practices that renew your energy from the inside out.

Body wisdom is your internal compass. Your body speaks to guide you, to protect you, and to remind you when you need softness or strength. When you listen to your body's signals, you learn when to slow down, when to nourish yourself, and when you are ready to bloom.

"Nourish to Flourish" encourages you to treat yourself as sacred soil. What you pour into yourself like love, rest, nourishment, and compassion directly shapes the woman you become. When you take care of your inner world, your outer world naturally begins to thrive.

BIBLE VERSE

Your Bible verse: _____

REFLECTION

_____

_____

_____

_____

_____

_____

_____

May

Nourish to Flourish

Theme: Self-care, restoration, body wisdom

1. What drains my energy the most and how can I protect it?

Today's date: _____

May

Nourish to Flourish

Theme: Self-care, restoration, body wisdom

2. How do I know when I'm running on empty?

Today's date: _____

WELLNESS JOURNAL

DATE: _____

MORNING ROUTINE:

- ☐ WAKE UP EARLY
- ☐ PRACTICE DEEP BREATHING FOR 3-5 MIN.
- ☐ HYDRATE WITH A GLASS OF WATER
- ☐ STRETCH

PHYSICAL ACTIVITY:

- ☐ ENGAGE IN 30 MINUTES OF EXERCISE
- ☐ TAKE SHORT WALKS OR STRETCH BREAKS
- ☐ USE THE STAIRS INSTEAD OF THE ELEVATOR
- ☐ TRACK DAILY STEPS

SELF-CARE:

- ☐ SET BOUNDARIES FOR YOUR PERSONAL TIME
- ☐ DO SOMETHING YOU ENJOY FOR AT LEAST 15 MIN.
- ☐ TAKE SHORT BREAKS TO RELAX
- ☐ DISCONNECT FROM SCREENS AT LEAST AN HOUR BEFORE BED

WATER INTAKE:

☐ ☐ ☐ ☐ ☐
☐ ☐ ☐ ☐ ☐

GRATITUDE:

- ☐ I'M GRATEFUL FOR MY HEALTH
- ☐ I APPRECIATE MY LOVED ONES
- ☐ I'M THANKFUL FOR LIFE
- ☐ I'M GRATEFUL FOR NEW OPPORTUNITIES

MINDFULNESS:

- ☐ 10 MINUTES OF MEDITATION
- ☐ GRATITUDE JOURNALING
- ☐ TAKE A FEW SOFT AND DEEP BREATHS
- ☐ MINDFUL EATING DURING MEALS

REFLECTION:

- ☐ REFLECT ON YOUR ACHIEVEMENTS TODAY
- ☐ NOTE ANY CHALLENGES
- ☐ HOW YOU OVERCAME THEM
- ☐ SET A SMALL WELLNESS GOAL FOR TOMOR

NUTRITION:

- ☐ EAT A BALANCED BREAKFAST
- ☐ PLAN HEALTHY MEALS FOR THE DAY
- ☐ SNACK ON FRUITS OR NUTS
- ☐ STAY HYDRATED THROUGHOUT THE DAY

NOTES:

- • _____
- • _____
- • _____

Take care of yourself first

Self Care Ideas

Spa day
Solo date
See a therapist
Read a book
Write in your journal
Run daily/weekly
Walk or go to the gym
Go to the hair salon or nail salon
Go on a date with a family or friend

date night

May

Nourish to Flourish

Theme: Self-care, restoration, body wisdom

3. What does true nourishment look like for my body, heart, and mind?

Today's date: _____

May

Nourish to Flourish

Theme: Self-care, restoration, body wisdom

4. What needs to be poured into me right now?

Today's date: _____

_____

_____

_____

_____

_____

_____

_____

_____

_____

_____

_____

_____

_____

_____

_____

_____

_____

_____

_____

_____

_____

_____

_____

May

Nourish to Flourish

Theme: Self-care, restoration, body wisdom

5. In what ways can I slow down and actually enjoy my life?

Today's date: _____

_____
_____
_____
_____
_____
_____
_____
_____
_____
_____
_____
_____
_____
_____
_____
_____
_____
_____
_____
_____
_____

Effective Action Plan

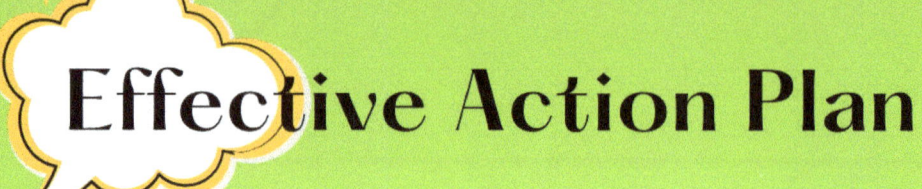

1. **Define Your Objectives**

2. **Set Your Goals**

3. **Prepare a Visual Plan**

4. **Assess Your Resources**

5. **Watch, Reflect, and Update**

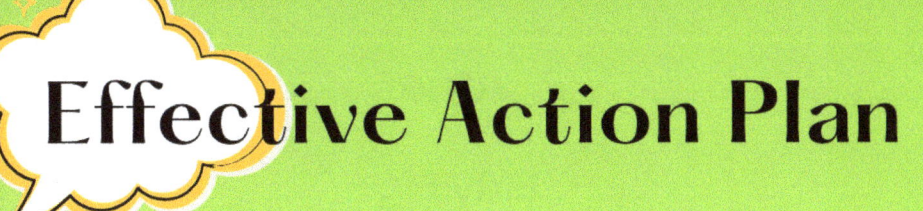

Effective Action Plan

June

Play Big

Theme: Boldness, Visibility, Empowerment

"Play Big" is a call to step into your full power without shrinking, doubting, or apologizing for your brilliance. It is the practice of owning your gifts, claiming space, and allowing yourself to be fully seen in a world that often teaches women to stay small.

Boldness is the courage to take risks, speak your truth, and pursue what lights you up even when fear whispers otherwise. Playing big means letting your actions match your potential instead of your insecurities.

Visibility is choosing to be seen and heard. It is no longer hiding your talents, your voice, or your dreams. When you play big, you stop dimming your light to make others comfortable. You show up with confidence, knowing that your presence matters.

Empowerment is the inner strength that grows as you choose yourself, again and again. It comes from breaking patterns of self-doubt, setting boundaries, and trusting your worth. Playing big is not about perfection, it's about stepping forward even when you feel unsure.

"Play Big" encourages you to stop waiting for permission. To stop minimizing your dreams. To stop acting like you are ordinary when you know you are extraordinary.

This is your reminder that your power expands when you use it, and your life expands when you dare to take up space.

BIBLE VERSE

Your Bible verse: _____

REFLECTION

_____

_____

_____

_____

_____

_____

_____

June

Play Big

Theme: Boldness, visibility, empowerment

1. What dream have I been quietly holding back?

Today's date: _____

June

Play Big

Theme: Boldness, visibility, empowerment

2. If I were fully confident, what would I go after?

Today's date: _____

WELLNESS JOURNAL

DATE: _____

MORNING ROUTINE:

- ☐ WAKE UP EARLY
- ☐ PRACTICE DEEP BREATHING FOR 3-5 MIN.
- ☐ HYDRATE WITH A GLASS OF WATER
- ☐ STRETCH

PHYSICAL ACTIVITY:

- ☐ ENGAGE IN 30 MINUTES OF EXERCISE
- ☐ TAKE SHORT WALKS OR STRETCH BREAKS
- ☐ USE THE STAIRS INSTEAD OF THE ELEVATOR
- ☐ TRACK DAILY STEPS

SELF-CARE:

- ☐ SET BOUNDARIES FOR YOUR PERSONAL TIME
- ☐ DO SOMETHING YOU ENJOY FOR AT LEAST 15 MIN.
- ☐ TAKE SHORT BREAKS TO RELAX
- ☐ DISCONNECT FROM SCREENS AT LEAST AN HOUR BEFORE BED

WATER INTAKE:

☐ ☐ ☐ ☐ ☐
☐ ☐ ☐ ☐ ☐

GRATITUDE:

- ☐ I'M GRATEFUL FOR MY HEALTH
- ☐ I APPRECIATE MY LOVED ONES
- ☐ I'M THANKFUL FOR LIFE
- ☐ I'M GRATEFUL FOR NEW OPPORTUNITIES

MINDFULNESS:

- ☐ 10 MINUTES OF MEDITATION
- ☐ GRATITUDE JOURNALING
- ☐ TAKE A FEW SOFT AND DEEP BREATHS
- ☐ MINDFUL EATING DURING MEALS

REFLECTION:

- ☐ REFLECT ON YOUR ACHIEVEMENTS TODAY
- ☐ NOTE ANY CHALLENGES
- ☐ HOW YOU OVERCAME THEM
- ☐ SET A SMALL WELLNESS GOAL FOR TOMOR

NUTRITION:

- ☐ EAT A BALANCED BREAKFAST
- ☐ PLAN HEALTHY MEALS FOR THE DAY
- ☐ SNACK ON FRUITS OR NUTS
- ☐ STAY HYDRATED THROUGHOUT THE DAY

NOTES:

- _____
- _____
- _____
  _____

Take care of yourself first

Self Care Ideas

Spa day
Solo date
See a therapist
Read a book
Write in your journal
Run daily/weekly
Walk or go to the gym
Go to the hair salon or nail salon
Go on a date with a family or friend

date night

June

Play Big

Theme: Boldness, visibility, empowerment

3. What limiting story am I ready to rewrite?

Today's date: _____

June

Play Big

Theme: Boldness, visibility, empowerment

4. Where am I ready to take up more space, within myself, in my energy, or in the actions I choose to take?

Today's date: _____

June

Play Big

Theme: Boldness, visibility, empowerment

5. What's one small step I can take toward a big goal?

Today's date: _____

_____

_____

_____

_____

_____

_____

_____

_____

_____

_____

_____

_____

_____

_____

_____

_____

_____

_____

_____

_____

_____

_____

Dice Brain Break

Roll a dice. The number that it lands on corresponds with the brain break activity!

 Dance for a one minute!

 Look in the mirror for two minutes!

Take three deep breaths!

Do four jumping jacks!

 Do five leg ups.

 Jog in place and count to 6.

Take care of yourself first

Self Care Ideas

Spa day
Solo date
See a therapist
Read a book
Write in your journal
Run daily/weekly
Walk or go to the gym
Go to the hair salon or nail salon
Go on a date with a family or friend

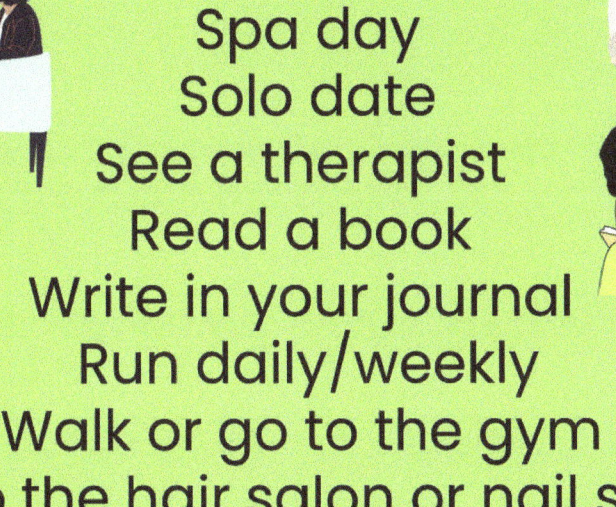
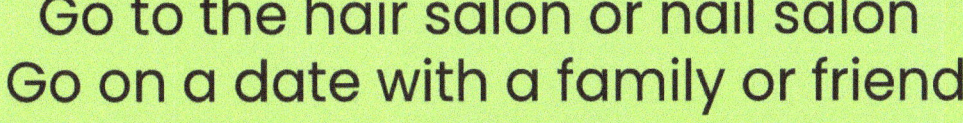

date night

Effective Action Plan

1 Define Your Objectives

2 Set Your Goals

3 Prepare a Visual Plan

4 Assess Your Resources

5 Watch, Reflect, and Update

Effective Action Plan

July

Feminine Flow

Theme: Intuition, Inner Guidance, Silence

"Feminine Flow" is the practice of moving through life with softness, trust, and alignment. It is the art of listening to your inner wisdom instead of forcing outcomes or pushing against your own natural rhythm. Feminine flow invites you to slow down enough to hear what your spirit is saying.

Intuition is the heartbeat of feminine flow. It's the quiet knowing that rises from within, the whisper that guides you toward what feels right and away from what drains your energy. When you honor your intuition, you begin making choices from a place of truth instead of fear.

Inner guidance is the steady voice that lives beneath the noise of the world. It speaks through sensations, emotions, and instinct. Feminine flow encourages you to trust this guidance, to believe that you already possess the answers you've been searching for externally.

Silence is the sacred space where clarity is born. In moments of stillness, away from distractions and expectations, you reconnect with yourself. Silence helps you soften your mind, open your heart, and hear the messages your intuition has been waiting to share.

"Feminine Flow" is not about passivity; it's about alignment. It's the practice of moving with ease, choosing with intention, and allowing life to unfold naturally. When you embrace feminine flow, you stop fighting the current and begin moving with it.

BIBLE VERSE

Your Bible verse: _____

REFLECTION

_____

_____

_____

_____

_____

_____

_____

July

Feminine Flow

Theme: : Intuition, inner guidance, silence

1. Where do I need to soften instead of push?

Today's date: _____

_____
_____
_____
_____
_____
_____
_____
_____
_____
_____
_____
_____
_____
_____
_____
_____
_____
_____
_____
_____
_____
_____
_____
_____
_____

July

Feminine Flow

Theme: : Intuition, inner guidance, silence

2. How does my body speak to me when something feels aligned or misaligned with my spirit? (Notice the sensations, peace, or tension that show up in silence.)

Today's date: _____

WELLNESS JOURNAL

DATE:

MORNING ROUTINE:

☐ WAKE UP EARLY
☐ PRACTICE DEEP BREATHING FOR 3-5 MIN.
☐ HYDRATE WITH A GLASS OF WATER
☐ STRETCH

PHYSICAL ACTIVITY:

☐ ENGAGE IN 30 MINUTES OF EXERCISE
☐ TAKE SHORT WALKS OR STRETCH BREAKS
☐ USE THE STAIRS INSTEAD OF THE ELEVATOR
☐ TRACK DAILY STEPS

SELF-CARE:

☐ SET BOUNDARIES FOR YOUR PERSONAL TIME
☐ DO SOMETHING YOU ENJOY FOR AT LEAST 15 MIN.
☐ TAKE SHORT BREAKS TO RELAX
☐ DISCONNECT FROM SCREENS AT LEAST AN
    HOUR BEFORE BED

WATER INTAKE:

GRATITUDE:

☐ I'M GRATEFUL FOR MY HEALTH
☐ I APPRECIATE MY LOVED ONES
☐ I'M THANKFUL FOR LIFE
☐ I'M GRATEFUL FOR NEW OPPORTUNITIES

MINDFULNESS:

☐ 10 MINUTES OF MEDITATION
☐ GRATITUDE JOURNALING
☐ TAKE A FEW SOFT AND DEEP BREATHS
☐ MINDFUL EATING DURING MEALS

REFLECTION:

☐ REFLECT ON YOUR ACHIEVEMENTS TODAY
☐ NOTE ANY CHALLENGES
☐ HOW YOU OVERCAME THEM
☐ SET A SMALL WELLNESS GOAL FOR TOMOR

NUTRITION:

☐ EAT A BALANCED BREAKFAST
☐ PLAN HEALTHY MEALS FOR THE DAY
☐ SNACK ON FRUITS OR NUTS
☐ STAY HYDRATED THROUGHOUT THE DAY

NOTES:

Take care of yourself first

Self Care Ideas

Spa day
Solo date
See a therapist
Read a book
Write in your journal
Run daily/weekly
Walk or go to the gym
Go to the hair salon or nail salon
Go on a date with a family or friend

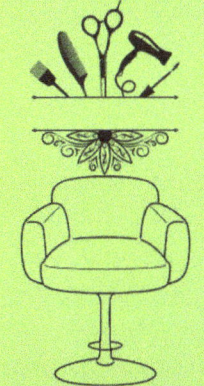

date night

July

Feminine Flow

Theme: : Intuition, inner guidance, silence

3. What is my body trying to communicate to me lately, and what steps can I take to honor its needs?

Today's date: _____

July

Feminine Flow

Theme: : Intuition, inner guidance, silence

4. What's the difference between fear and intuition for me?

Today's date: _____

July

Feminine Flow

Theme: : Intuition, inner guidance, silence

5. What inner wisdom is calling for my attention and asking me to listen?

Today's date: _____

Share your Thoughts

Effective Action Plan

1 Define Your Objectives

2 Set Your Goals

3 Prepare a Visual Plan

4 Assess Your Resources

5 Watch, Reflect, and Update

Effective Action Plan

August

Inner Flame

Theme: Passion, Purpose, Creative Fire

Your Inner Flame is the spark within you, the energy that makes you feel alive, driven, and connected to something bigger than yourself. It is the glowing center of your passion, the whisper of your purpose, and the heat that fuels your creativity.

Passion is the fire that lights you up from the inside. It's the excitement you feel when you're doing what you love, the joy that pulls you forward, and the emotional energy that makes your life feel meaningful. Your inner flame grows stronger every time you honor what excites your spirit.

Purpose is the direction your flame points toward. It's the deeper calling behind your gifts, experiences, and desires. When you connect with your purpose, your inner flame becomes a guiding light, giving meaning to the challenges you overcome and clarity to the path ahead.

Creative fire is the expression of your inner flame. It's your ability to imagine, build, express, and bring new ideas into the world. This creative energy is limitless when you allow yourself to dream boldly and create without self-judgment.

Your Inner Flame is your truth, your spark, your life force. It reminds you that you are powerful, capable, and full of potential. When you tend to this flame, through authenticity, joy, and alignment, you become unstoppable.

BIBLE VERSE

Your Bible verse: _____

REFLECTION

_____

_____

_____

_____

_____

_____

_____

August

Inner Flame

Theme: Passion, purpose, creative fire

1. What am I deeply passionate about and do I honor it?

Today's date: _____

August

Inner Flame

Theme: Passion, purpose, creative fire

2. When was the last time I felt lit up from within?

Today's date: _____

WELLNESS JOURNAL

DATE: _____

MORNING ROUTINE:
- [ ] WAKE UP EARLY
- [ ] PRACTICE DEEP BREATHING FOR 3-5 MIN.
- [ ] HYDRATE WITH A GLASS OF WATER
- [ ] STRETCH

PHYSICAL ACTIVITY:
- [ ] ENGAGE IN 30 MINUTES OF EXERCISE
- [ ] TAKE SHORT WALKS OR STRETCH BREAKS
- [ ] USE THE STAIRS INSTEAD OF THE ELEVATOR
- [ ] TRACK DAILY STEPS

SELF-CARE:
- [ ] SET BOUNDARIES FOR YOUR PERSONAL TIME
- [ ] DO SOMETHING YOU ENJOY FOR AT LEAST 15 MIN.
- [ ] TAKE SHORT BREAKS TO RELAX
- [ ] DISCONNECT FROM SCREENS AT LEAST AN HOUR BEFORE BED

WATER INTAKE:

GRATITUDE:
- [ ] I'M GRATEFUL FOR MY HEALTH
- [ ] I APPRECIATE MY LOVED ONES
- [ ] I'M THANKFUL FOR LIFE
- [ ] I'M GRATEFUL FOR NEW OPPORTUNITIES

MINDFULNESS:
- [ ] 10 MINUTES OF MEDITATION
- [ ] GRATITUDE JOURNALING
- [ ] TAKE A FEW SOFT AND DEEP BREATHS
- [ ] MINDFUL EATING DURING MEALS

REFLECTION:
- [ ] REFLECT ON YOUR ACHIEVEMENTS TODAY
- [ ] NOTE ANY CHALLENGES
- [ ] HOW YOU OVERCAME THEM
- [ ] SET A SMALL WELLNESS GOAL FOR TOMORR

NUTRITION:
- [ ] EAT A BALANCED BREAKFAST
- [ ] PLAN HEALTHY MEALS FOR THE DAY
- [ ] SNACK ON FRUITS OR NUTS
- [ ] STAY HYDRATED THROUGHOUT THE DAY

NOTES:
_____
- _____
- _____
- _____

Take care of yourself first

Self Care Ideas

Spa day
Solo date
See a therapist
Read a book
Write in your journal
Run daily/weekly
Walk or go to the gym
Go to the hair salon or nail salon
Go on a date with a family or friend

date night

August

Inner Flame

Theme: Passion, purpose, creative fire

3. What have I been called to create, say, or share?

Today's date: _____

_____
_____
_____
_____
_____
_____
_____
_____
_____
_____
_____
_____
_____
_____
_____
_____
_____
_____
_____
_____
_____
_____
_____
_____

August

Inner Flame

Theme: Passion, purpose, creative fire

4. How do I align with my deeper purpose?

Today's date: _____

August

Inner Flame

Theme: Passion, purpose, creative fire

5. What am I burning to change in myself or the world?

Today's date: _____

Effective Action Plan

1. Define Your Objectives

2. Set Your Goals

3. Prepare a Visual Plan

4. Assess Your Resources

5. Watch, Reflect, and Update

Effective Action Plan

September

Wholeness

Theme: Reflection, resilience, wisdom

Wholeness is about embracing every part of yourself: your strengths, your challenges, your past, and your growth. It's the process of recognizing that you are complete and valuable, even in moments of struggle or imperfection.

- Reflection: Wholeness begins with looking inward honestly examining your experiences, feelings, and choices without judgment.

- Resilience: It involves acknowledging setbacks or wounds and understanding that they don't define you; they are part of your journey toward strength.

- Wisdom: Wholeness grows as you learn from life's lessons, integrate them, and move forward with understanding, compassion, and clarity.

Wholeness reminds you that you are complete as you are, and that every part of your story contributes to your power, beauty, and authenticity. Take time in this journal to explore, reflect, and reconnect with the fullness of who you are.

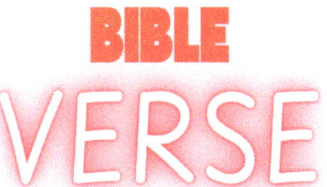

BIBLE VERSE

Your Bible verse: _____

REFLECTION

_____

_____

_____

_____

_____

_____

_____

September

Wholeness

Theme: Reflection, resilience, wisdom

1. What challenge taught me the most this year?

Today's date: _____

September

Wholeness

Theme: Reflection, resilience, wisdom

2. How has pain or struggle helped shape my strength?

Today's date: _____

_____
_____
_____
_____
_____
_____
_____
_____
_____
_____
_____
_____
_____
_____
_____
_____
_____
_____
_____
_____
_____
_____
_____
_____
_____

Share your Thoughts

WELLNESS JOURNAL

DATE: ....

MORNING ROUTINE:

- [ ] WAKE UP EARLY
- [ ] PRACTICE DEEP BREATHING FOR 3-5 MIN.
- [ ] HYDRATE WITH A GLASS OF WATER
- [ ] STRETCH

PHYSICAL ACTIVITY:

- [ ] ENGAGE IN 30 MINUTES OF EXERCISE
- [ ] TAKE SHORT WALKS OR STRETCH BREAKS
- [ ] USE THE STAIRS INSTEAD OF THE ELEVATOR
- [ ] TRACK DAILY STEPS

SELF-CARE:

- [ ] SET BOUNDARIES FOR YOUR PERSONAL TIME
- [ ] DO SOMETHING YOU ENJOY FOR AT LEAST 15 MIN.
- [ ] TAKE SHORT BREAKS TO RELAX
- [ ] DISCONNECT FROM SCREENS AT LEAST AN
      HOUR BEFORE BED

WATER INTAKE:

GRATITUDE:

- [ ] I'M GRATEFUL FOR MY HEALTH
- [ ] I APPRECIATE MY LOVED ONES
- [ ] I'M THANKFUL FOR LIFE
- [ ] I'M GRATEFUL FOR NEW OPPORTUNITIES

MINDFULNESS:

- [ ] 10 MINUTES OF MEDITATION
- [ ] GRATITUDE JOURNALING
- [ ] TAKE A FEW SOFT AND DEEP BREATHS
- [ ] MINDFUL EATING DURING MEALS

REFLECTION:

- [ ] REFLECT ON YOUR ACHIEVEMENTS TODAY
- [ ] NOTE ANY CHALLENGES
- [ ] HOW YOU OVERCAME THEM
- [ ] SET A SMALL WELLNESS GOAL FOR TOMOR

NUTRITION:

- [ ] EAT A BALANCED BREAKFAST
- [ ] PLAN HEALTHY MEALS FOR THE DAY
- [ ] SNACK ON FRUITS OR NUTS
- [ ] STAY HYDRATED THROUGHOUT THE DAY

NOTES:

- ....
- ....
- ....

Take care of yourself first

Self Care Ideas

Spa day
Solo date
See a therapist
Read a book
Write in your journal
Run daily/weekly
Walk or go to the gym
Go to the hair salon or nail salon
Go on a date with a family or friend

date night

September

Wholeness

Theme: Reflection, resilience, wisdom

3. What's a past version of me that I now feel gratitude for?

Today's date: _____

_____
_____
_____
_____
_____
_____
_____
_____
_____
_____
_____
_____
_____
_____
_____
_____
_____
_____
_____
_____
_____
_____
_____
_____
_____

September

Wholeness

Theme: Reflection, resilience, wisdom

4. What lesson keeps repeating itself in my life?

Today's date: _____

September

Wholeness

Theme: Reflection, resilience, wisdom

5. What has life been trying to teach me based on my experiences?

Today's date: _____

Effective Action Plan

1 Define Your Objectives

2 Set Your Goals

3 Prepare a Visual Plan

4 Assess Your Resources

5 Watch, Reflect, and Update

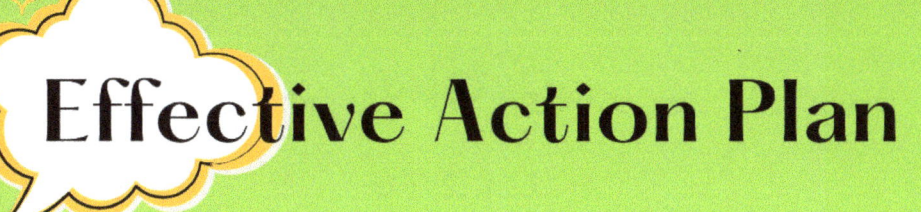

Effective Action Plan

October

Let It Go

Theme: Release, forgiveness, emotional decluttering

Let It Go is about freeing yourself from what no longer serves you. It's the conscious choice to release anger, resentment, guilt, or past hurts so that your mind, heart, and spirit have space to heal and thrive.

- Release: Let go of heavy emotions, situations, or expectations that weigh you down.

- Forgiveness: Allow yourself and others the grace to move beyond mistakes, misunderstandings, and regrets.

- Emotional Decluttering: Clear mental and emotional clutter to make room for peace, clarity, and joy.

Letting go doesn't mean forgetting or condoning, it means choosing your own freedom and creating space for growth, self-love, and inner calm.

BIBLE VERSE

Your Bible verse: _____

REFLECTION

_____

_____

_____

_____

_____

_____

_____

October

Let It Go

Theme: Release, forgiveness, emotional decluttering

1. What am I still carrying that no longer serves me?

Today's date: ———————————

October

Let It Go

Theme: Release, forgiveness, emotional decluttering

2. Who or what am I still holding resentment toward?

Today's date: _____

WELLNESS JOURNAL

DATE:

MORNING ROUTINE:

- [ ] WAKE UP EARLY
- [ ] PRACTICE DEEP BREATHING FOR 3-5 MIN.
- [ ] HYDRATE WITH A GLASS OF WATER
- [ ] STRETCH

PHYSICAL ACTIVITY:

- [ ] ENGAGE IN 30 MINUTES OF EXERCISE
- [ ] TAKE SHORT WALKS OR STRETCH BREAKS
- [ ] USE THE STAIRS INSTEAD OF THE ELEVATOR
- [ ] TRACK DAILY STEPS

SELF-CARE:

- [ ] SET BOUNDARIES FOR YOUR PERSONAL TIME
- [ ] DO SOMETHING YOU ENJOY FOR AT LEAST 15 MIN.
- [ ] TAKE SHORT BREAKS TO RELAX
- [ ] DISCONNECT FROM SCREENS AT LEAST AN HOUR BEFORE BED

WATER INTAKE:

GRATITUDE:

- [ ] I'M GRATEFUL FOR MY HEALTH
- [ ] I APPRECIATE MY LOVED ONES
- [ ] I'M THANKFUL FOR LIFE
- [ ] I'M GRATEFUL FOR NEW OPPORTUNITIES

MINDFULNESS:

- [ ] 10 MINUTES OF MEDITATION
- [ ] GRATITUDE JOURNALING
- [ ] TAKE A FEW SOFT AND DEEP BREATHS
- [ ] MINDFUL EATING DURING MEALS

REFLECTION:

- [ ] REFLECT ON YOUR ACHIEVEMENTS TODAY
- [ ] NOTE ANY CHALLENGES
- [ ] HOW YOU OVERCAME THEM
- [ ] SET A SMALL WELLNESS GOAL FOR TOMOR

NUTRITION:

- [ ] EAT A BALANCED BREAKFAST
- [ ] PLAN HEALTHY MEALS FOR THE DAY
- [ ] SNACK ON FRUITS OR NUTS
- [ ] STAY HYDRATED THROUGHOUT THE DAY

NOTES:

Take care of yourself first

Self Care Ideas

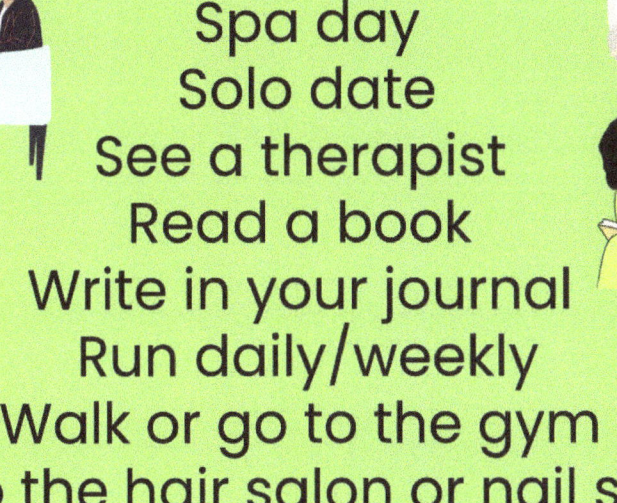

Spa day
Solo date
See a therapist
Read a book
Write in your journal
Run daily/weekly
Walk or go to the gym
Go to the hair salon or nail salon
Go on a date with a family or friend

date night

October

Let It Go

Theme: Release, forgiveness, emotional decluttering

3. What outdated story or label do I need to let go of?

Today's date: _____

_____

_____

_____

_____

_____

_____

_____

_____

_____

_____

_____

_____

_____

_____

_____

_____

_____

_____

_____

_____

_____

October

Let It Go

Theme: Release, forgiveness, emotional decluttering

4. What emotion needs space to move through me?

Today's date: _____

_____
_____
_____
_____
_____
_____
_____
_____
_____
_____
_____
_____
_____
_____
_____
_____
_____
_____
_____
_____
_____
_____
_____
_____

October

Let It Go

Theme: Release, forgiveness, emotional decluttering

5. How can I feel lighter in my heart and mind?

Today's date: _____

Effective Action Plan

1 Define Your Objectives

2 Set Your Goals

3 Prepare a Visual Plan

4 Assess Your Resources

5 Watch, Reflect, and Update

Effective Action Plan

November

Devotion

Theme: Discipline, sacred living, grounding

Devotion is the act of showing up for yourself and your life with intention and care. It's about nurturing your goals, values, and spirit through consistent, mindful practice. By embracing discipline, you honor your commitments; through sacred living, you recognize the beauty and purpose in each moment; and by staying grounded, you remain connected to your truth and inner strength.

- Discipline: Devotion requires commitment, focus, and the willingness to stay consistent even when it's challenging.

- Sacred Living: It's about honoring your life, your body, and your choices as acts of reverence, treating everyday moments as meaningful.

- Grounding: Devotion keeps you centered, rooted in your truth, and aligned with what nourishes your soul.

Devotion is more than action, it's a lifestyle of love, focus, and presence that transforms ordinary days into meaningful practice.

BIBLE VERSE

Your Bible verse: _____

REFLECTION

_____

_____

_____

_____

_____

_____

November

Devotion

Theme: Discipline, sacred living, grounding

1. What am I truly devoted to in this season of life?

Today's date: _____

_____
_____
_____
_____
_____
_____
_____
_____
_____
_____
_____
_____
_____
_____
_____
_____
_____
_____
_____
_____
_____
_____

Share your Thoughts

November

Devotion

Theme: Discipline, sacred living, grounding

2. What daily routine helps me return to myself?

Today's date: _____

WELLNESS JOURNAL

DATE:

MORNING ROUTINE:

- [ ] WAKE UP EARLY
- [ ] PRACTICE DEEP BREATHING FOR 3-5 MIN.
- [ ] HYDRATE WITH A GLASS OF WATER
- [ ] STRETCH

PHYSICAL ACTIVITY:

- [ ] ENGAGE IN 30 MINUTES OF EXERCISE
- [ ] TAKE SHORT WALKS OR STRETCH BREAKS
- [ ] USE THE STAIRS INSTEAD OF THE ELEVATOR
- [ ] TRACK DAILY STEPS

SELF-CARE:

- [ ] SET BOUNDARIES FOR YOUR PERSONAL TIME
- [ ] DO SOMETHING YOU ENJOY FOR AT LEAST 15 MIN.
- [ ] TAKE SHORT BREAKS TO RELAX
- [ ] DISCONNECT FROM SCREENS AT LEAST AN HOUR BEFORE BED

WATER INTAKE:

GRATITUDE:

- [ ] I'M GRATEFUL FOR MY HEALTH
- [ ] I APPRECIATE MY LOVED ONES
- [ ] I'M THANKFUL FOR LIFE
- [ ] I'M GRATEFUL FOR NEW OPPORTUNITIES

MINDFULNESS:

- [ ] 10 MINUTES OF MEDITATION
- [ ] GRATITUDE JOURNALING
- [ ] TAKE A FEW SOFT AND DEEP BREATHS
- [ ] MINDFUL EATING DURING MEALS

REFLECTION:

- [ ] REFLECT ON YOUR ACHIEVEMENTS TODAY
- [ ] NOTE ANY CHALLENGES
- [ ] HOW YOU OVERCAME THEM
- [ ] SET A SMALL WELLNESS GOAL FOR TOMORR

NUTRITION:

- [ ] EAT A BALANCED BREAKFAST
- [ ] PLAN HEALTHY MEALS FOR THE DAY
- [ ] SNACK ON FRUITS OR NUTS
- [ ] STAY HYDRATED THROUGHOUT THE DAY

NOTES:

Take care of yourself first

Self Care Ideas

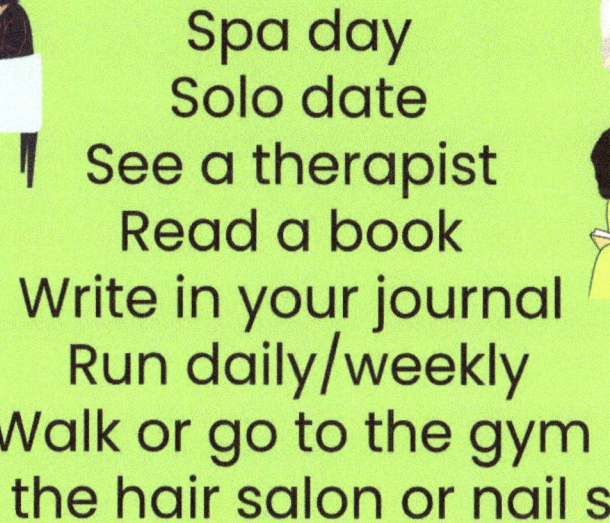

Spa day
Solo date
See a therapist
Read a book
Write in your journal
Run daily/weekly
Walk or go to the gym
Go to the hair salon or nail salon
Go on a date with a family or friend

date night

November

Devotion

Theme: Discipline, sacred living, grounding

3. How can I deepen my relationship with the divine (however I define it)?

Today's date: _____

_____

_____

_____

_____

_____

_____

_____

_____

_____

_____

_____

_____

_____

_____

_____

_____

_____

_____

_____

_____

_____

_____

November

Devotion

Theme: Discipline, sacred living, grounding

4. What does a sacred life look like to me?

Today's date: _____

_____
_____
_____
_____
_____
_____
_____
_____
_____
_____
_____
_____
_____
_____
_____
_____
_____
_____
_____
_____
_____

Share your Thoughts

November

Devotion

Theme: Discipline, sacred living, grounding

5. In what ways can I make my everyday routines feel more sacred and intentional?

Today's date: _____

Effective Action Plan

1 Define Your Objectives

2 Set Your Goals

3 Prepare a Visual Plan

4 Assess Your Resources

5 Watch, Reflect, and Update

Effective Action Plan

December

Integration

Theme: Reflection, honoring the journey, wholeness

Integration is the art of bringing all aspects of yourself, your experiences, lessons, and emotions, into balance. It's about honoring every step of your journey, learning from your challenges, and celebrating your growth. When you integrate your past and present, you cultivate wholeness, clarity, and inner harmony.

- Reflection: Pause to look back on your experiences and understand their impact on your growth.

- Honoring the Journey: Recognize the lessons, efforts, and milestones that have brought you to this moment.

- Wholeness: Integration weaves together your past, present, and aspirations so you can move forward feeling balanced, empowered, and aligned.

In essence, integration is about embracing your entire story. Through reflection and self-awareness, integration helps you move forward with confidence, fully aligned with who you are meant to be.

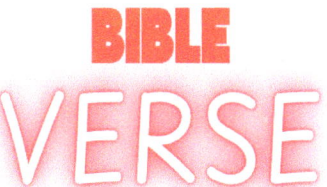

BIBLE VERSE

Your Bible verse: _____

REFLECTION

_____

_____

_____

_____

_____

_____

_____

December

Integration

Theme: Reflection, honoring the journey, wholeness

1. How have I changed this year?

Today's date: _____

December

Integration

Theme: Reflection, honoring the journey, wholeness

2. How have my greatest challenges shaped me, and what wisdom did they teach me?

Today's date: _____

WELLNESS JOURNAL

DATE:

MORNING ROUTINE:

- ☐ WAKE UP EARLY
- ☐ PRACTICE DEEP BREATHING FOR 5 MINUTES
- ☐ HYDRATE WITH A GLASS OF WATER
- ☐ STRETCH OR DO A QUICK YOGA SESSION

GRATITUDE:

- ☐ I'M GRATEFUL FOR MY HEALTH
- ☐ I APPRECIATE MY LOVED ONES
- ☐ I'M THANKFUL FOR LIFE'S SIMPLE PLEASURES
- ☐ I'M GRATEFUL FOR NEW OPPORTUNITIES

PHYSICAL ACTIVITY:

- ☐ ENGAGE IN 30 MINUTES OF EXERCISE
- ☐ TAKE SHORT WALKS OR STRETCH BREAKS
- ☐ USE THE STAIRS INSTEAD OF THE ELEVATOR
- ☐ TRACK DAILY STEPS OR DISTANCE

MINDFULNESS:

- ☐ PRACTICE 10 MINUTES OF MEDITATION
- ☐ PRACTICE GRATITUDE JOURNALING
- ☐ TAKE A FEW MOMENTS TO BREATHE DEEPLY
- ☐ MINDFUL EATING DURING MEALS

SELF-CARE:

- ☐ SET BOUNDARIES FOR WORK AND PERSONAL TIME
- ☐ DO SOMETHING YOU ENJOY FOR AT LEAST 15 MINUTES
- ☐ TAKE SHORT BREAKS TO RELAX OR DO A QUICK HOBBY
- ☐ DISCONNECT FROM SCREENS AT LEAST AN HOUR BEFORE BED

REFLECTION:

- ☐ REFLECT ON YOUR ACHIEVEMENTS TODAY
- ☐ NOTE ANY CHALLENGES AND HOW YOU OVERCAME THEM
- ☐ CONSIDER WHAT YOU'RE GRATEFUL FOR TODAY
- ☐ SET A SMALL WELLNESS GOAL FOR TOMORROW

WATER INTAKE:

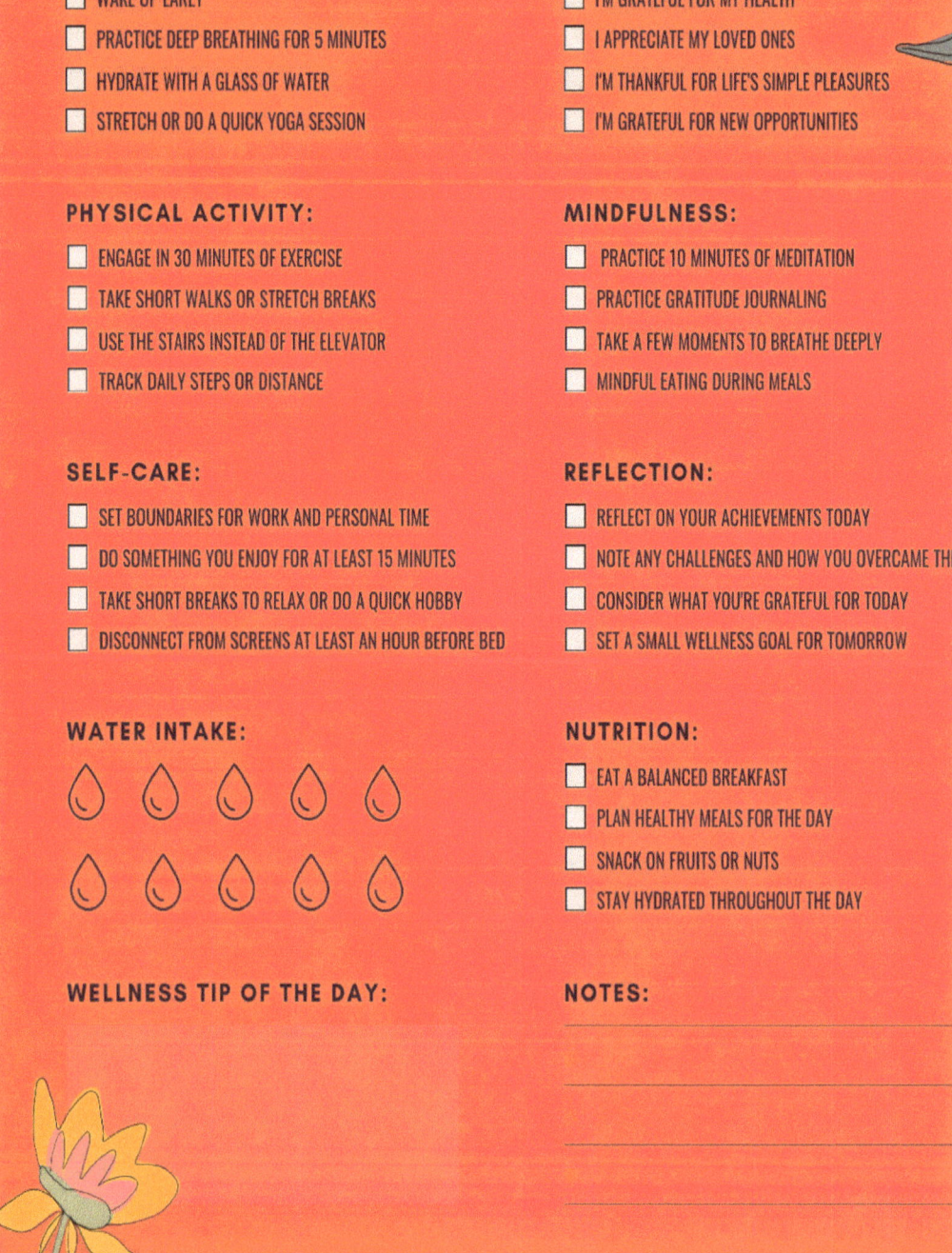

NUTRITION:

- ☐ EAT A BALANCED BREAKFAST
- ☐ PLAN HEALTHY MEALS FOR THE DAY
- ☐ SNACK ON FRUITS OR NUTS
- ☐ STAY HYDRATED THROUGHOUT THE DAY

WELLNESS TIP OF THE DAY:

NOTES:

Take care of yourself first

Self Care Ideas

Spa day
Solo date
See a therapist
Read a book
Write in your journal
Run daily/weekly
Walk or go to the gym
Go to the hair salon or nail salon
Go on a date with a family or friend

date night

December

Integration

Theme: Reflection, honoring the journey, wholeness

3. What parts of myself am I ready to welcome and embrace more deeply?

Today's date: _____

_____
_____
_____
_____
_____
_____
_____
_____
_____
_____
_____
_____
_____
_____
_____
_____
_____
_____
_____
_____
_____
_____
_____

December

Integration

Theme: Reflection, honoring the journey, wholeness

4. What will I release, and what will I take with me into the future?

Today's date: _____

_____
_____
_____
_____
_____
_____
_____
_____
_____
_____
_____
_____
_____
_____
_____
_____
_____
_____
_____
_____

December

Integration

Theme: Reflection, honoring the journey, wholeness

5. In what ways have I embodied the power within, and how can I continue to step into that power more fully?

Today's date: _____

Effective Action Plan

1 Define Your Objectives

2 Set Your Goals

3 Prepare a Visual Plan

4 Assess Your Resources

5 Watch, Reflect, and Update

Effective Action Plan

Final Affirmation

I am healed.

I am whole.

I am loved.

I flourish in peace, in purpose, and in legacy.

When you complete this journal, email Ruth to share a testimony. Wish you all the best. Blessings & love!

S.o.tpublishing@gmail.com

www.ingramcontent.com/pod-product-compliance
Lightning Source LLC
Chambersburg PA
CBHW051146120626
46547CB00012B/966